BEST OF MARCH MADNESS

STUNNING MARCH MADNESS UPSETS

BY CHARLIE BEATTIE

abdobooks.com

Published by Abdo Publishing, a division of ABDO, PO Box 398166, Minneapolis, Minnesota 55439.

Printed in the United States of America, North Mankato, Minnesota.
102025
012026

Cover Photos: Dylan Buell/Getty Images Sport/Getty Images, Jared C. Tilton/Getty Images Sport/Getty Images, LM Otero/AP Images
Interior Photos: Otto Greule Jr./Allsport/Getty Images Sport/Getty Images, 4–5; Mitchell Layton/Getty Images Sport/Getty Images, 7; Grant Halverson/NCAA Photos/Getty Images, 9; Rich Clarkson/NCAA Photos/Getty Images, 10–11, 28–29, 31, 39; Roberto Borea/AP Images, 12; Tom Russo/AP Images, 14; Joe Imel/AP Images, 17; Tim Nwachukwu/Getty Images Sport/Getty Images, 19; Doug Mills/AP Images, 20–21; Dave Martin/AP Images, 23; Eric Gay/AP Images, 25; Paul Sakuma/AP Images, 26; Mark Cornelison/Lexington Herald-Leader/Tribune News Service/Getty Images, 33; Justin Tafoya/NCAA Photos/Getty Images, 34; Ronald C. Modra/Getty Images Sport/Getty Images, 36–37; Gary Landers/AP Images, 40; Elsa/Getty Images Sport/Getty Images, 42; Mark Humphrey/AP Images, 44; Lance King/Getty Images Sport/Getty Images, 45

Editor: Dalton Rains
Series Designer: Ebonee Estrella

Library of Congress Control Number: 2025939874

Publisher's Cataloging-in-Publication Data

Names: Beattie, Charlie, author.
Title: Stunning March Madness upsets / by Charlie Beattie
Description: Minneapolis, Minnesota: Abdo Publishing, 2026 | Series: Best of March Madness | Includes online resources and index.
Identifiers: ISBN 9781098298203 (lib. bdg.) | ISBN 9798384932000 (ebook)
Subjects: LCSH: Basketball--Juvenile literature. | College sports--Juvenile literature. | Basketball--Tournaments--United States--Juvenile literature. | College sports--United States--History--Juvenile literature. | NCAA Basketball Tournament--Juvenile literature. | March Madness (National Collegiate Athletic Association)--Juvenile literature.
Classification: DDC 796.32363--dc23

TABLE OF CONTENTS

STANFORD
10

CHAPTER ONE

SLAYING GIANTS

On paper, the 1998 matchup between No. 1 seed Stanford and No. 16 seed Harvard was a huge mismatch. Legendary Stanford head coach Tara VanDerveer and the Cardinal had played in the previous three women's Final Fours. Harvard had only ever played in the National Collegiate Athletic Association (NCAA) Tournament twice. In addition, the game was being played on Stanford's home court.

Stanford also had history on its side. The men's NCAA Tournament had expanded to 64 teams in 1985. The women's tournament did the same in 1994. In that time, a No. 1 seed had never been upset by a No. 16 seed in either tournament.

Cardinal fans were confident. As Harvard's players took the court for the first time, they were greeted by hecklers. "Welcome to real basketball," one fan called out.

Tara VanDerveer, *right*, became Stanford's head coach in 1985.

Unlike Stanford's fans, Coach VanDerveer did not underestimate Harvard. Senior forward Allison Feaster led the nation with 28.5 points per game for the Crimson that season. Meanwhile, the Cardinal had lost two of their best scorers to knee injuries. VanDerveer was prepared for a tough battle.

Stanford fans were in for a harsh awakening. At halftime, Harvard led 43–34. The Cardinal rallied and snatched a 65–62 lead with just under three minutes left in the game. But Harvard didn't fold. The Crimson made a layup to cut Stanford's lead to one. The Cardinal came up empty in their next possession. Back at Harvard's end of the court, Feaster fed a pass to teammate Suzie Miller. The junior guard-forward's jump shot rattled in and the Crimson regained the lead.

After another Stanford miss, freshman guard Lisa Kowal tore down the court. She split two Cardinal defenders before spotting Miller open in the corner. Miller drained a three-pointer to put Harvard up 69–65 with 46 seconds left. Stanford never recovered. Feaster finished with 35 points as Harvard won 71–67.

ENDING THE STREAK

Virginia was one of the strongest teams in the 2018 men's NCAA Tournament field. Powered by a solid defense, the Cavaliers came into the tournament with a

Virginia guard Kyle Guy averaged a team-high 14.1 points per game in 2017–18.

31–2 record and the top overall seed. All season long, they had jumped out to early leads and stifled opponents' comeback attempts.

In the 33 years since the men's tournament expanded to 64 teams, No. 1 seeds were 132–0. Fans expected Virginia to keep the streak alive. The Cavaliers' game was one of the last first-round matchups to tip off. Their opponent was the University of Maryland, Baltimore County (UMBC). UMBC had barely clinched a spot in the 2018 tournament. With less than a second left in the

UMBC guard Jairus Lyles (10) scored a game-high 28 points against Virginia.

Retrievers' conference tournament final, guard Jairus Lyles hit a game-winning three to earn the berth.

Both teams struggled to get into a rhythm in the first half. At halftime, the score was 21–21. Then the Retrievers came out of the locker room hot. Guard Joe Sherburne completed a three-point play just 25 seconds into the second half. On UMBC's next possession, the junior drilled a three-pointer. With 16:24 left, he hit another three to put the Retrievers up 35–24. Then, after a Virginia turnover, Lyles was fouled while attempting another deep shot. The senior guard hit all three of his free throws to increase the lead to 14 points. Virginia fans were completely stunned.

The Cavaliers were used to gradually imposing their will on opponents. They weren't built to make big comebacks. It didn't help that the Retrievers finished the game with 12 three-pointers. In just the second half, they scored 53 points against a Virginia defense that, on average, gave up 53 points per game. With each shot, it dawned on more fans and players that history was being made. The final buzzer made it official. UMBC clinched a 74–54 win.

GIANT KILLERS

In the opening round of the 2023 NCAA Tournament, Zach Edey of top-seeded Purdue towered over the roster of No. 16 seed Fairleigh Dickinson (FDU). The 7-foot-4 center had won the Naismith Trophy as the best men's player in the nation. Meanwhile, no FDU player was taller than 6-foot-7. Nonetheless, the Knights stunned the Boilermakers in the first-round matchup. Despite 21 points from Edey, FDU won 63–58 to become the third No. 16 seed to advance to the second round.

NAVY
50

CHAPTER TWO

EARLY-ROUND MAGIC

The 1985 men's NCAA tournament was the first to feature 64 teams. That year's opening round also featured a shocking upset. No. 13 seed Navy had a dominant player in center David Robinson. The future National Basketball Association (NBA) superstar led Navy against heavily favored Louisiana State University (LSU). The No. 4 seed Tigers had no answers for Robinson. He finished the game with 18 points, 18 rebounds, and three blocks. Navy stunned LSU 78–55.

A few years later, another future NBA star faced an underdog matchup. Entering the 1993 men's NCAA tournament, few fans had heard of Steve Nash. And even fewer thought the Canadian point guard's

In 1985, Navy center David Robinson posted a total of 40 points and 26 rebounds over two tournament games.

Santa Clara guards Mark Schmitz (20) and Steve Nash (11) celebrate a 64–61 upset over Arizona.

No. 15 Santa Clara Broncos could beat No. 2 seed Arizona in the first round.

Coming off the bench, Nash hit only one field goal all game. However, using his tight ballhandling skills, the freshman kept possessions alive and controlled the pace of the game while setting up teammates with slick passes.

Late in the game, Santa Clara protected a small lead. Arizona began intentionally fouling, and Nash usually had the ball. He had eight free-throw attempts in the final two minutes. He made the first six. But with six seconds remaining, Nash missed two shots that could have put the game away.

The Broncos grabbed the rebound on the second miss. Arizona fouled another Santa Clara freshman, Kevin Dunne. But Dunne also missed both of his free throws. After the second, Arizona star Damon Stoudamire grabbed the long rebound. He heaved up a shot in desperation, but the ball clanked off the rim. Santa Clara's 64–61 upset was complete.

THE BACKDOOR CUT

Legendary coach Pete Carril arrived at Princeton in 1967. Carril's final season with the team was 1995–96. That year, he led the Tigers to the men's NCAA Tournament for the 11th time. Most fans thought it would be a short stay. The No. 13 seed Tigers were up against defending national champion University of California, Los Angeles (UCLA), in the first round.

The athletic Bruins had five players who averaged in double figures that season. Princeton had only one.

But Carril's team also used an effective strategy, fittingly named "The Princeton Offense." The Tigers began possessions with all five players outside the arc. The four players without the ball moved and cut constantly. The idea was to wait for the perfect shot, which often came

Princeton guard Mitch Henderson scored eight points and dished out three assists against UCLA.

from a player making a backdoor cut for an open layup. The openings took time to develop, so the slow style often resulted in low-scoring games.

That pace frustrated UCLA. Entering the final minute, the score was 41–41. The Tigers grabbed a rebound off a Bruins miss. Then Carril called timeout with 21 seconds left to set up a final play. After a handful of passes, Princeton got the ball to center Steve Goodrich at the free-throw line. Meanwhile, guard Gabe Lewullis was stationed on the right wing. He faked a backdoor cut, then drifted back out. When the guard's defender came to meet him, Lewullis darted to the basket again. Goodrich fed the freshman a perfect bounce pass, and Lewullis laid it in with 3.9 seconds to go. UCLA missed its final shot. Princeton pulled off a 43–41 upset for the final win of Carril's legendary coaching career.

NO SURE THING

Pat Summitt coached Tennessee from 1974 to 2012. The Lady Volunteers won eight national titles in that time. Even when they didn't win it all, the team always seemed to make deep runs. There was little reason to expect otherwise in the 2009 women's NCAA Tournament.

The No. 5 Lady Vols were two-time defending national champions. Under Summitt, they had a record of 42–0 in the first two rounds. Few thought No. 12 seed Ball State would change that. In contrast to the veteran Summitt, Cardinals coach Kelly Packard was in her first season. And this was Ball State's first-ever NCAA tournament.

Even still, the Ball State players appeared comfortable and prepared for the moment. The Cardinals' guards sped around defenders. Ball State held on to a one-point lead into halftime.

Things got worse for the young Tennessee team in the second half. Starting center Kelley Cain left the game with an injury. Meanwhile, Ball State guards Porchia Green and Audrey McDonald carved up Tennessee's defense. Green scored a game-high 23 points. McDonald added 18. The Cardinals were just as effective on defense. They forced 16 turnovers and held Tennessee to 34.8 percent shooting. The underdogs pulled away for a 71–55 win. Ball State didn't win another game in the tournament, and Packard coached there for just three more seasons. But for one day, she got the best of a coaching legend.

FROM DEEP

In the first round of the 2024 men's NCAA Tournament, No. 14 seed Oakland faced No. 3 Kentucky. The Golden Grizzlies hadn't been to the tournament in more than a decade. In fact, most fans were surprised to find out that the small school isn't in Oakland, California. It is actually in Oakland County, Michigan.

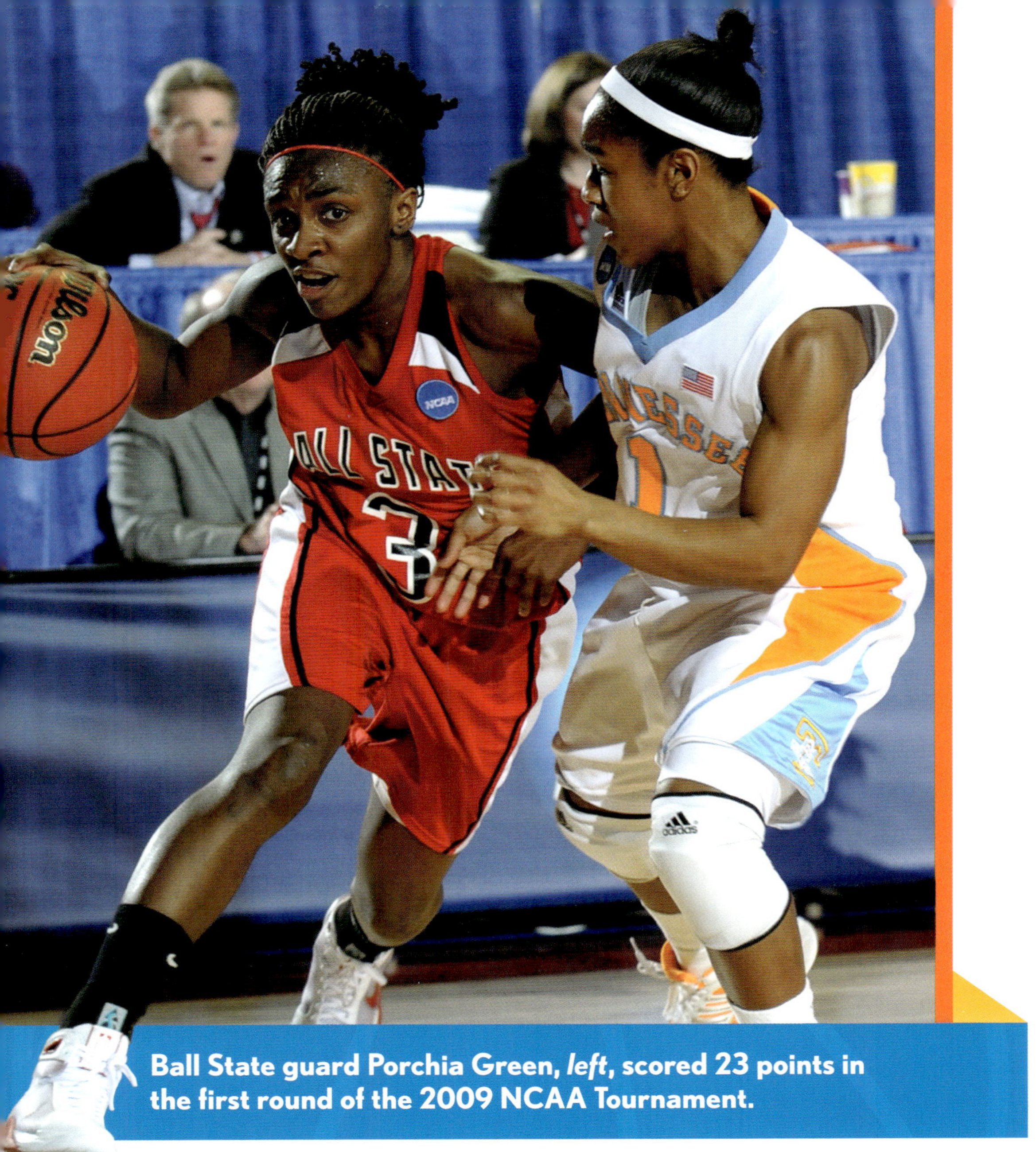

Ball State guard Porchia Green, *left*, scored 23 points in the first round of the 2009 NCAA Tournament.

The Golden Grizzlies' second-leading scorer was Jack Gohlke, a 6-foot-3 senior who had been playing Division II basketball just a year earlier. Gohlke was a pure three-point shooter. Entering the NCAA Tournament, the guard had taken 335 shots. Only eight of them had come from inside the arc.

With just over 13 minutes left in the first half, Gohlke hit an off-balance shot from the left wing. Soon after, he came off a screen and launched another deep fadeaway three. It rattled in to give Oakland an 11–9 lead.

Gohlke hit five more three-pointers in the first half. Each one seemed more unlikely than the last. His final shot of the half came 1:55 before the break. The senior banked it in from several feet behind the three-point line.

The game stayed close through the second half. With under five minutes to go, the Golden Grizzlies held a 64–62 lead. Gohlke caught a pass on the left wing.

BEWARE THE 12s

Ever since the men's NCAA Tournament expanded to 64 teams in 1985, No. 12 seeds have been particularly dangerous. In 2025, both Colorado State and McNeese State won first-round games as No. 12 seeds. That meant at least one No. 12 seed had won in 34 of the previous 40 tournaments. It was also the 18th time that multiple No. 12 seeds had pulled first-round upsets.

Guard Jack Gohlke (3) shot 50 percent from three-point range in Oakland's 2024 first-round matchup.

Shooting over a lunging defender, he made his 10th three-pointer of the game.

Gohlke finished the game with a career-high 32 points. Oakland won 80–76. It was just the second NCAA Tournament win ever for the school. Kentucky forward Tre Mitchell summed up the upset by simply saying, "It's March."

25
44

CHAPTER THREE

UPSET SPECIALISTS

By 1991, the University of Richmond men's team had built up a résumé of upsets. In 1984, the Spiders were a No. 12 seed when they stunned No. 5 Auburn 72–71 in the first round. Four years later, Richmond was seeded No. 13. The Spiders took down defending champion Indiana 72–69.

Now a No. 15 Richmond team opened the 1991 NCAA Tournament against No. 2 Syracuse. In the first six seasons of the 64-team tournament, No. 15 seeds were 0–24. Unbothered, Richmond finished the first half with a 44–36 lead. Syracuse fought back in the second. Richmond's lead was just 70–69 in the final minute of the game. Then Richmond guard Eugene Burroughs was fouled. As the freshman stepped to the line, he spotted his father

Richmond forward Kenny Wood (44) grabbed seven rebounds in the first round of the 1991 men's NCAA Tournament.

pumping his fist in the crowd. Burroughs winked back. He then sank both shots.

Syracuse had one last chance to tie the game. But the three-pointer rolled off the rim. Richmond took possession. After being fouled, Curtis Blair sank a free-throw to seal the 73–69 upset.

Richmond didn't get back to the NCAA Tournament until 1998. That year, the No. 14 seed Spiders matched up against No. 3 seed South Carolina. With a 62–61 win, Richmond became first school to win games as a No. 12, No. 13, No. 14, and No. 15 seed.

THE SHOW

The No. 3 seed Michigan State Spartans were a little too confident heading into the 1995 men's NCAA Tournament. They faced No. 14 seed Weber State. When asked about the small school from Ogden, Utah, several Spartans said they didn't know where it was.

Michigan State led by nine at halftime. But then the Wildcats surged behind guard Ruben Nembhard's 27 points. They emerged with a 79–72 win.

In 1999, Weber State was a No. 14 seed once again. This time, the Wildcats went up against North Carolina. The Tar Heels hadn't lost an opening game since 1980.

Junior forward Harold Arceneaux was Weber State's biggest star. He averaged 22.3 points per game in

1998–99. However, with the Wildcats playing in the small Big Sky Conference, the forward didn't get much national attention.

Over the course of two hours, Arceneaux became the talk of the NCAA Tournament. He scored 36 points. During one stretch in the second half, he scored 11 straight points for the Wildcats.

Arceneaux mixed deep shots with crafty drives. But his most important shots were free throws. With 13 seconds left, he drained two from the line to put Weber State up 75–72. The Wildcats hung on for a 76–74 win.

BLUE RAIDED

Entering the 2004 women's NCAA Tournament, coach Sylvia Hatchell's North Carolina hadn't lost in the first

Weber State players celebrate after upsetting Michigan State in the 1995 men's NCAA Tournament.

round since 1985. Meanwhile, the Middle Tennessee Blue Raiders didn't have much of a postseason history. The No. 13 seed had made the field for the first time since 1998. Middle Tennessee had won only one tournament game ever. Even so, junior forward Patrice Holmes helped the Blue Raiders build a lead against North Carolina. She finished with a game-high 18 points. The underdogs had a 12-point lead with under seven minutes remaining in the second half.

North Carolina rallied and had a chance to tie the game late. With 34 seconds to go, Middle Tennessee held on to a two-point lead. Tar Heels center Candace Sutton's layup attempt rolled off the rim, and the Blue Raiders grabbed the rebound. North Carolina went scoreless for the rest of the game, and Middle Tennessee won 67–62.

A year later, Middle Tennessee made it back to the tournament as a No. 12 seed. This time, the Blue Raiders squared off against North Carolina State (NC State). Just like the year before, Holmes lifted Middle Tennessee to a lead. However, NC State surged ahead in the second half, and Holmes had to help the Blue Raiders crawl back.

The game was tied 58–58 in the final seconds. Holmes came off a screen and curled to the middle of the lane. Guard Chrissy Givens fed the Blue Raiders star a pass. Holmes then hit a 10-foot jumper with 1.6 seconds left. Middle Tennessee won 60–58.

Middle Tennessee guard Patrice Holmes celebrates after scoring a game-winner in the 2005 women's NCAA Tournament.

OUTFOXED

In 2007, Marist entered the women's NCAA Tournament as a No. 13 seed. The small New York school had roughly 6,000 students. The Red Foxes faced Ohio State, which was nearly 10 times larger.

Marist players turned their attention to Buckeyes star Jessica Davenport, a 6-foot-5 center who entered the matchup averaging 20 points per game. The defenders forced the senior into

Guard Julianne Viani scored 13 points in Marist's second-round upset over Middle Tennessee in 2007.

11 turnovers. On the other end, Red Foxes guard Julianne Viani hit six three-pointers. Her hot shooting helped Marist erase a four-point halftime deficit. With under 10 seconds to play, Nikki Flores knocked down two free throws to put Marist up 67–63. Then Ohio State missed a three-point attempt with four seconds remaining. The Red Foxes' upset was complete.

In 2012, Marist was once again a No. 13 seed. Stellar shooting gave the Red Foxes a five-point halftime lead over No. 4 Georgia. Even after the Bulldogs went ahead in the second half, Marist answered with a rally of its own. Down 62–61 with under four minutes to go, the Red Foxes put together eight unanswered points to help them clinch a 76–70 win. At the time, only six No. 13 seeds had ever won a first-round game in the NCAA women's tournament. Marist had done it twice.

MARIST VS. MIDDLE TENNESSEE

After beating Ohio State in the 2007 women's tournament, Marist took on Middle Tennessee in the second round. The No. 5 seed Blue Raiders weren't an underdog anymore. It was their turn to be on the losing side of an upset. Marist pulled another stunner, winning 73–59.

STATE
44
53

CHAPTER FOUR

FINAL FOUR UPSETS

In 1974, NC State's men's team was strong. Coach Norm Sloan's Wolfpack won the Atlantic Coast Conference (ACC) tournament. But there was no doubt who the favorite was, and that team was waiting for NC State in the Final Four.

Coach John Wooden's UCLA Bruins had won six NCAA Championships in a row. Many thought they would win again in 1974. The Wolfpack had other plans. Led by double-doubles from stars David Thompson and Tom Burleson, NC State dueled UCLA into double overtime. With just under a minute to go, Thompson banked in a shot to put the Wolfpack up 76–75. The team hung on for a memorable 80–77 upset. Two days later, NC State beat Marquette to win the program's first national title.

NC State guard David Thompson averaged 24.3 points per game in the 1974 men's NCAA Tournament.

REVENGE ON THE REBELS

In 1990, Duke met the University of Nevada, Las Vegas (UNLV), in the men's national title game. The Runnin' Rebels buried Duke 103–73. It was the biggest blowout in NCAA men's championship-game history.

Few predicted a different result when the teams met a year later in the Final Four. UNLV entered the game on a 45-game winning streak. The Runnin' Rebels were expected to become the first undefeated champion since 1976. Meanwhile, Duke had yet to break through to win a national title.

The teams slugged back and forth all game. With less than a minute to go, the score was 77–77. Duke's Thomas Hill missed a jump shot. But the Blue Devils' star center Christian Laettner battled for the rebound. He was fouled with 12 seconds left, leading to two huge free throws. He looked over to coach Mike Krzyzewski and confidently said, "I got `em."

Laettner hit both shots, but UNLV still had one more chance. Fans expected UNLV forward Larry Johnson to take the last shot. Johnson surprised many by passing to teammate Anderson Hunt. Hunt's three-point attempt bounced off the rim, and Duke point guard Bobby Hurley grabbed the rebound as time expired. The Blue Devils had pulled off an incredible upset on the way to their first national title.

Christian Laettner scored 28 points in the 1991 men's NCAA Tournament semifinals.

ALMOST PERFECT

In the 2010s, Kentucky coach John Calipari often led the most loaded teams in men's basketball. Calipari was a master when it came to recruiting "one-and-done" players. These talented freshmen would stay in college for only one season before heading to the pros.

Calipari assembled one of his most talented groups in 2014–15. Led by four elite freshmen, including future NBA stars Devin Booker and Karl-Anthony Towns, Kentucky rolled into the Final Four 38–0. The Wildcats hoped to become the first undefeated NCAA champion in 39 years.

Despite a 35–3 record and a No. 1 seed, Wisconsin was an underdog. The Badgers were led by older players, such as junior forward Sam Dekker and senior center Frank Kaminsky. They would have to rely on experience and effort to upset fellow No. 1 Kentucky.

The teams were an even match in the first half. Then Wisconsin surged to a 52–44 lead early in the second half, thanks to the shooting of Dekker, Kaminsky, and point guard Bronson Koenig. However, the Badgers went cold after that run. Over the next 10 minutes, they hit only one field goal. Wisconsin's strong defense was all that kept the Badgers in the game.

The score was 60–60 with under two minutes left. Dekker dribbled near the top of the key. After jabbing

Wisconsin center Frank Kaminsky had two blocks in the 2015 NCAA men's semifinals.

toward the basket to shake his defender, the junior stepped back and hit a clutch three-pointer. Although Kentucky closed to within a point in the final minute, the Badgers held on. Wisconsin scored its final eight points at the free-throw line and claimed a 71–64 victory.

ENDING THE STREAK

Entering the 2017 women's Final Four, the UConn Huskies were on the most dominant run in college basketball history. Coach Geno Auriemma's team hadn't lost a game since November of 2014. The Huskies' 111-game winning streak was 21 games longer than the second-longest streak, which UConn also held.

Mississippi State guard Morgan William, *left*, scored 13 points in the 2017 women's national championship.

UConn faced Mississippi State in the 2017 Final Four. A year earlier, the teams had met in the Sweet 16. UConn had steamrolled the Bulldogs 98–38.

This year, however, Mississippi State point guard Morgan William was on a tear. The 5-foot-5 junior had erupted for 41 points to beat Baylor in the Elite Eight, setting up the matchup with UConn.

The Bulldogs took a surprise 36–28 lead heading into halftime. But UConn rallied to tie the game heading into the fourth quarter. Still tied with time running out, William drove to the basket. But UConn forward Gabby Williams swatted away her shot to force overtime.

The teams were deadlocked 64–64 in the final seconds of the overtime period. After a UConn turnover, William took a feed from Bulldogs guard Dominique Dillingham and sprinted into the lane. Once again, UConn's Williams was defending the paint. With one second on the clock, the Mississippi State guard pulled up at the elbow. Her high-arcing shot went over Williams's hand and dropped through the net as time expired.

Two nights later, the Bulldogs lost to South Carolina in the title game. But William's game-winner is still the lasting memory of the 2017 NCAA Tournament.

CLARK SHOOTS DOWN SOUTH CAROLINA

As a No. 2 seed, Iowa may not have been a traditional underdog in the 2023 Final Four against South Carolina. However, the No. 1 seed Gamecocks entered the game 36–0. Many fans thought the defending champions would keep the streak going in the semifinals. Iowa star guard Caitlin Clark had other plans. She drilled five three-pointers on her way to a 41-point, eight-assist performance. The Hawkeyes upset the Gamecocks 77–73 to snap South Carolina's 42-game winning streak.

CHAPTER FIVE

CHAMPIONSHIP UPSETS

The 1983 men's national title game looked like a huge mismatch. NC State was a solid team and the ACC Tournament champion. But the Wolfpack was just a No. 6 seed in that year's NCAA Tournament. Despite the middling seed, coach Jim Valvano's group had made an unexpected run to the national championship game. The intimidating No. 1 seed Houston Cougars were waiting.

Coach Guy Lewis's fast-paced Houston teams thrilled fans through the early 1980s. The Cougars were loaded with talent, including future Hall of Famers Clyde Drexler and Akeem (later known as Hakeem) Olajuwon. The Cougars were dubbed "Phi Slama Jama" because of their rim-rattling dunks.

Coach Jim Valvano's NC State Wolfpack went 26–10 in the 1982–83 season.

Valvano knew his team's only chance was to slow the game down. At the time, college basketball didn't use a shot clock. If the Wolfpack could keep the ball away from Houston's high-pressure defense, they could run the clock down on every possession. That strategy worked throughout the first half. Led by the steady play of point guard Dereck Whittenburg, NC State headed into halftime with a 33–25 lead.

All tournament long, the Wolfpack had been known as the "Cardiac Pack" for its close games. After erasing a six-point Houston lead in the final three minutes of the game, the team was headed for another nail-biter.

NC State had the ball with 44 seconds left, and Valvano called timeout to set up a final play. However, the play did not go as planned. Houston stretched out its defense and gambled for steals on nearly every pass. NC State nearly turned the ball over twice. With under 10 seconds left, Whittenburg had to chase down a loose ball near midcourt. As he turned, he knew he had to get a shot up.

Whittenburg launched a shot from 35 feet. It was an air ball. But waiting under the basket was 6-foot-7 NC State forward Lorenzo Charles. The sophomore caught the ball just short of the rim, immediately slamming it through the hoop. The buzzer-beater clinched the biggest championship upset the NCAA had seen yet.

NC State forward Lorenzo Charles slams down the championship-winning dunk in 1983.

THE PERFECT GAME

Two years after NC State's improbable win, there seemed to be another huge championship-game mismatch. The Georgetown Hoyas and Villanova Wildcats met in the 1985 men's title game. Both teams played in the Big East Conference, but that was about all they had in common that season.

The Hoyas were the defending national champions. And the No. 1 seed had the nation's most dominant player in 7-foot center Patrick Ewing. Villanova, meanwhile, had struggled through the season and entered the tournament

Forward Ed Pinckney celebrates after scoring 16 points in Villanova's 1985 men's national championship victory.

as a No. 8 seed. The Wildcats needed a string of upsets to reach the final.

Villanova and Georgetown had played twice during the regular season. The games were close, but Georgetown won both. Few thought the third meeting would be any different. To many, the only question entering the game was how badly Villanova would be beaten. One national newspaper previewed the game with the headline "Villanova vs. a god."

Despite the expectations, the Wildcats gave Georgetown trouble from the start. On defense, Villanova pressured and frustrated Ewing. On offense, the Wildcats couldn't miss. Just as NC State had two years earlier, Villanova thrived without a shot clock. Point guard Gary McLain dribbled circles around Georgetown's defense while his teammates got open. The Wildcats came through with the performance of the season, shooting a tournament-record 79 percent from the field.

Even with that hot shooting, Georgetown stayed in the game. The teams traded the lead nine times in the second half. But Villanova surged ahead late and held a two-point lead in the final seconds. The Wildcats just had to run out the clock. Guard Harold Jensen was looking for forward Dwayne McClain on the inbound pass. But McClain got tangled up with his defender. Both players went to the floor, but Jensen noticed that McClain was actually still open. Jensen threw the ball in, and McClain caught the pass while lying on his stomach. Cradling the ball in his right arm, he threw his left in the air as time ran out. Villanova had pulled off an incredible upset. Forty years later, the Wildcats were still the lowest seed to ever win the tournament.

AGGIES UPSET

Entering the 2011 women's NCAA Tournament, 12 of the previous 16 titles had been won by either UConn or Tennessee. Both teams entered the 2011 field as

No. 1 seeds. But when No. 2 seed Notre Dame beat both powerhouses on its way to the title game, the Fighting Irish became the team to beat.

On the other side of the bracket, Texas A&M was also a No. 2 seed. The Aggies beat the other two No. 1s, Baylor and Stanford, on the way to the final. But in an unlikely title matchup, Texas A&M was seen as the more surprising team.

The Aggies stunned the Fighting Irish with fierce defense early on. Texas A&M built a 29–16 lead before Notre Dame star Skylar Diggins dragged her team back into the game. In the second half, it was back and forth through the final minutes.

DANNY AND THE MIRACLES

In 1988, No. 6 seed Kansas was the third unlikely men's champion of the decade. The team was led by superstar senior Danny Manning. Known as "Danny and the Miracles," Kansas had to get by No. 1 Oklahoma in the championship game. Oklahoma had won both regular-season matchups between the conference rivals. But Manning scored 31 points, grabbed 18 rebounds, and added five steals as Kansas won the title matchup 83–79.

Danielle Adams scored 30 points in Texas A&M's 2011 NCAA Championship win over Notre Dame.

Diggins hit a short floater to tie the game 66–66 with just under four minutes left. But Aggies stars Danielle Adams and Tyra White took over from there. Adams scored the next four points. Then, with the score at 70–68 and just over a minute left, White rose over Diggins and hit a clutch three-pointer.

The Aggies knocked down free throws to finish out a 76–70 win. In a tournament that had always been dominated by the favorites, the Aggies were perhaps the unlikeliest champion in women's basketball history.

HONORABLE MENTIONS

TEXAS A&M VS. FLORIDA (1994)

No. 13 Texas A&M caught a lucky break in the 1994 women's NCAA Tournament. High seeds usually got to play at home, but Florida's arena was being used for a concert. So the Aggies played their first-round matchup in Texas. Texas A&M point guard Lisa Branch sank two free throws to seal a 78–76 win, making the Aggies the first No. 13 seed to win a women's tournament game.

HAMPTON VS. IOWA STATE (2001)

Hampton is a small school from southeast Virginia. The No. 15 seed took on No. 2 seed Iowa State in the first round of the 2001 men's tournament. Pirates forward Tarvis Williams sank a jump shot with 6.9 seconds left to give Hampton a 58–57 win.

Janel McCarville

MINNESOTA VS. DUKE (2004)

In 2004, No. 7 Minnesota put together a run to the women's Elite Eight. Facing No. 1 seed Duke, Minnesota stars Lindsay Whalen and Janel McCarville carried the team. Whalen led all scorers with 27 points. McCarville added 20 points and 18 rebounds. Minnesota's 82–75 victory marked the first time the school had ever beaten a No. 1 seed.

NORFOLK STATE VS. MISSOURI AND LEHIGH VS. DUKE (2012)

Entering the 2012 men's tournament, only four No. 15 seeds had ever won in the first round. In a matter of hours, two more pulled off stunning upsets. First, Norfolk State center Kyle O'Quinn completed a three-point play in the final minute to help the Spartans beat Missouri 86–84. Later, Duke struggled to contain Lehigh star guard C. J. McCollum. The future NBA standout torched the Blue Devils for 30 points as Lehigh won 75–70.

C. J. McCollum

WRIGHT STATE VS. ARKANSAS (2021)

Wright State had never won an NCAA Tournament game. But the No. 13 seed Raiders hung with No. 4 seed Arkansas into the final minutes of their first-round matchup in the 2021 women's tournament. Raiders guard Angel Baker knocked down a three-pointer with 29 seconds left to seal Wright State's 66–62 victory.

NORTH CAROLINA VS. DUKE (2022)

The 2022 season was the last in the legendary career of Duke men's coach Mike Krzyzewski. When the No. 2 seed Blue Devils reached the Final Four, it looked as if "Coach K" would go out by winning his sixth national championship. But Duke's biggest rival spoiled the ending. Though the Tar Heels were just a No. 8 seed, guard Caleb Love scored a game-high 28 points to snatch an upset win.

GLOSSARY

assist
A pass that leads directly to a basket.

conference
A group of schools that join together to create a league for their sports teams.

deficit
The amount by which a team is trailing in a game.

double-double
Accumulating 10 or more of two certain statistics in a game.

elbow
The area on a basketball court where the free-throw line meets the lane line.

inbound
To pass a ball inbounds to begin a possession.

recruiting
Convincing a high school player to attend a certain college, usually to play sports.

rivals
Teams or players that have a fierce and ongoing competition against one another.

screen
A legal block made by an offensive player against a defender to open up a teammate for a shot or a pass.

seed
A rank assigned to a player or team in a tournament.

turnover
The act of losing possession of the ball.

MORE INFORMATION

BOOKS

Big Book of Who Women in Sports: The 101 Stars Every Fan Needs to Know. Triumph, 2025.

Giedd, Steph. *Basketball Strategies*. Abdo, 2024.

Hanlon, Luke. *Everything Basketball*. Abdo, 2025.

ONLINE RESOURCES

To learn more about stunning March Madness upsets, please visit **abdobooklinks.com** or scan this QR code. These links are routinely monitored and updated to provide the most current information available.

INDEX

ABOUT THE AUTHOR

Charlie Beattie is a writer, editor, and former sportscaster. Originally from Saint Paul, Minnesota, he now lives in Charleston, South Carolina, with his wife and son.